Somerset County
A Millennial Portrait

Photography

Walter Choroszewski

Introduction

Governor Christine Todd Whitman

Published in cooperation with

Somerset Alliance for the Future

Published by

Aesthetic Press, Inc.

Somerville, New Jersey

Dedicated to the people of Somerset County.

Somerset County, A Millennial Portrait

Edited and designed by Walter Choroszewski.
Printed in China - First Printing 1999.

ISBN 0-933605-09-9

Walter Choroszewski

As a photographer, author and lecturer, Walter Choroszewski has been presenting the best of New Jersey since 1980, and has published numerous books and calendars on the state. Walter, his wife, Susan, son, Joe, and their English Springer Spaniel, "Beans," live in the village of South Branch.

Aesthetic Press, Inc.

Box 5306, Somerville, NJ 08876-1303   Tel: 908 369-3777

Opposite - Rudolf W. van der Goot Rose Garden,
Colonial Park Arboretum, Franklin.
Overleaf - Farm silhouette, South Branch.

Somerset

Somerset County is like home to me, and for a good part of my life, it was home.

Reflecting on the years that I spent there—first as a young mother raising two children, later as a public official—I can't help but look fondly at those bygone days. Scenic bike trips along the towpath of the Delaware and Raritan Canal. Meeting citizens on the steps of the historic Somerset County Court House. Patriotic parades from enchanting Raritan to Victorian North Plainfield. Hot air balloons floating over farmers' fields on sleepy Sunday mornings. These are among my most cherished memories.

I know I can recapture these feelings by going back to Somerset County even now, as we enter the new millennium.

That is the true beauty of Somerset. Because it has managed to hold on to its loveliness and charm, future generations can look forward to the same simple pleasures I enjoyed. The small-town feel of Bound Brook. Picturesque Somerville. The rural charm of Montgomery. The horse farms of Bedminster. Fishing on the banks of the Raritan River. Sweeping views of the Manhattan skyline from Washington Rock Park. All can be found within the boundaries of Somerset County.

Thanks to an aggressive open space program Somerset County boasts more than 7,300 acres of pristine parkland. It is no wonder Somerset County regularly lands on the lists of America's best places to live.

But beyond Somerset's beauty is its historic significance and the richness of its past. One of the nation's oldest counties, Somerset is steeped in colonial and Revolutionary War history. Virtually every one of its 21 municipalities takes note of its important historical past. The county is studded with historic sites and monuments. Rockingham near Rocky Hill, where General George Washington stayed while he attended sessions of the Continental Congress in 1734. The Wallace House in Somerville, which served as Washington's headquarters from the winter of 1778 to the summer of 1779. Middlebrook, where the first 13-star flag of our nation was raised over the Continental troops encamped there under General Washington's command.

Patriotism runs rampant within the county—no place stronger than at the Manville VFW Post 2290, where WWII veteran John Pavuk tells his stories of the Battle of the Bulge. Raritan, too, remembers its war heroes— like John Basilone, a United States Marine who earned the Medal of Honor for his bravery at Guadalcanal.

Somerset is truly proud of this rich history. Volunteerism runs high with groups like The Heritage Trail Association and The Meadows Foundation which are active in preserving and sharing the county's historic sites for generations to come. Margaret Chandler Nevius, who turns 108 this year, still remembers when barges plied the Delaware & Raritan Canal. Over the last half century she has actively volunteered her time for the preservation of the Blackwells Mills Canal House in Franklin.

Somerset County was initially settled by the Dutch in the 17th century— proof found in the countless white steeples of the Dutch Reformed churches that dot the county's landscape. Today it is a place where people from many corners of the world have found a home. Restaurants along Main Street in Somerville offer a plethora of varied ethnic cuisines. Raritan Valley Community College celebrates this diversity each year at its annual International Festival.

Indeed, Somerset County is a picture of the American dream, and now it has widened its embrace to take in the Great American Pastime. Former New York Yankee pitching legend Sparky Lyle is the manager of the new Somerset County Patriots baseball team. Sparky will tell you there's no finer arena for his young ball team than the new Somerset County Ballpark in Bridgewater.

Somerset County, centrally located, was a crossroads in colonial times and remains so, even today, with highways 22, 287, and 78. But cars still stop on South Branch Road every morning and evening to allow the cows a safe crossing to the other side. Bicycles traverse the county's parks and country roads, and each Memorial Day weekend, people come from around the world to participate in the celebrated Tour of Somerville bicycle races.

Photographer Walter Choroszewski lives in Somerset County. He's made a career of showcasing New Jersey with his beautiful imagery. With this book, as with all of his work, Choroszewski has truly captured the loveliness and character of a place that he holds near and dear, as I do.

I would like to commend Somerset Alliance for the Future and The Heritage Trail Association for their parts in promoting this project and for their strong commitment to maintaining the county's high quality of life.

*As you turn the pages of **Somerset County, A Millennial Portrait**, drink in Walter Choroszewski's enchanting scenes of the county, and feel the pride that is shared by all who know and love Somerset County.*

Christine Todd Whitman
Governor
State of New Jersey

Above - Dawn, Branchburg.

Left - Barn, Montgomery.

Opposite - Barn, Far Hills.

Val Kreutler with the

4-H Poultry Club, Bridgewater.

Above - South Branch School

House. 1873. Branchburg.

Right - Pete Quick,

farmer. Hillsborough.

Left - Spring farmscape,

Hillsborough.

Opposite - Van Wickle

House Garden,

Franklin.

Above - Spring pathway,

Leonard J. Buck Gardens, Far Hills.

Opposite - Spring display, The French

Garden, Duke Gardens, Hillsborough.

Above - Aerial of bridges over Raritan River, Neshanic.

Top - Bridge detail, Neshanic.

Left - Conrail freight tracks, Hillsborough.

Opposite Right - NJ Transit railyard, Gladstone.

Opposite Top - Aerial of crossroads of

Routes 287 and 78, Bedminster.

Above - Biking through Raritan.

Left - Trophy, U.S. Bicycling
Hall of Fame, Somerville.

Right - Oldest bicycle race in
America, Tour of Somerville.

Above - Aerial, Bridgewater Commons.

Left - Mall queens, Melissa and Sara,

Bridgewater Commons, Bridgewater.

Above - The Neshanic

Flea Market, Branchburg.

Right - Rail Road Junction

Flea Market, Bound Brook.

Above - Warrenbrook Golf Course, Warren and Green Brook.

Top - Fiddlers Elbow Country Club, Bedminster.

Right - U.S. Golf Association Museum and Library, Far Hills.

The Old Filter House,

Nevius Street, Raritan.

Live chess match,

The New Jersey

Renaissance

Kingdom, Somerset.

Above - Fishing, Delaware & Raritan Canal, Franklin.

Top Right - Fishing, Delaware & Raritan Canal, South Bound Brook.

Fishing, Raritan River, Raritan.

Above - Artist, Wayne Mathisen,
painting the Bridge at Opie's Mill, Montgomery.
Opposite - The dam at Ravine Lake, Far Hills.

Above - Four Oaks

Farm, Branchburg.

Left - Hillsborough.

Top Left - Bedminster.

Above - Canada geese,
Watchung Lake,
Watchung.
Left - Great Blue Heron,
Duke Island Park,
Bridgewater.

Branta Pond, Environmental Education Center,

Lord Stirling Park. Basking Ridge.

Above - Washington Park Historic District, North Plainfield.

Opposite - South Branch Historic District, Hillsborough.

Hot air balloons

float over South Branch.

"Mountain Dew"
balloon drifts over a
Branchburg farm.

Above - Clock tower,

Pharmacia-Upjohn,

Peapack & Gladstone.

Right - North Plainfield.

The Coach Barn, Duke Estate, Hillsborough.

Above - Morning "Cow Crossing,"

South Branch Road, Branchburg.

Left - Stanley & David Kanach.

River-Lea Farm, Branchburg.

Top Left - Aerial of

River-Lea Farm, Branchburg.

Above - Horse farm,

Branchburg.

Left - Raritan River, Manville.

Left - Chief of Police,

Richard Voorhees,

Bridgewater.

Above - Friday Cruise Night,

Main Street, Somerville.

Right - Monday Cruise Night,

Main Street, Bound Brook.

Moggy Brook, Leonard J. Buck Gardens, Far Hills.

Above - Statue of Metropolitan Wasyl Lypkiwsky,

St. Andrew's Ukranian Memorial Cathedral,

South Bound Brook.

Left - Millicent Fenwick statue, Bernardsville.

General Cornwallis,

Franklin Inn, Franklin.

General Washington.

Washington Rock State Park,

Green Brook.

Fields along
the Raritan River.
Branchburg and
Hillsborough.

Essex Fox Hounds,

Peapack & Gladstone.

WEST END HOSE, 1888

RELIEF 2 HOSE

FIREMEN'S MUSEUM

Above - Relief Hose,
firehouse sign, Raritan.
Left - Firemen's Museum,
Somerville.

Above - Young firefighters,

River Park, Bedminster.

Right - Neshanic.

Far Right - Firemen's

Memorial, North Plainfield.

Above & Right - Old Dutch Parsonage, Somerville.

Opposite - Cross Estate Gardens, Bernardsville.

Ukranian dancers,
International Festival,
Raritan Valley
Community College,
Branchburg.

Criollo Sentir dancer,
International Festival,
Raritan Valley
Community College,
Branchburg.

Warrenbrook Senior Center, Warren.

Above - Blackwells Mills
Canal House, Franklin.
Left - Born in 1892,
Margaret Chandler Nevius,
lifelong volunteer
for Blackwells Mills
Canal House and The
Meadows Foundation.

Right - Hotel Somerset,
Somerville.
Opposite - New York
City skyline view from
Washington Rock State
Park, Green Brook.

Participants in

Special Olympics,

Bridgewater:

Above - Kyle Osterloh.

Right - Jayne McGuigan.

Opposite - Charlie Morgan.

Van Dorn Mill,

Franklin Corners

Historic District,

Bernards Township.

Mount St. Mary's Academy, Watchung.

Above - Harlingen Reformed
Church, Montgomery.
Right - Hillsborough
Reformed Church, Millstone.

Above - North Branch
Reformed Church,
Bridgewater.

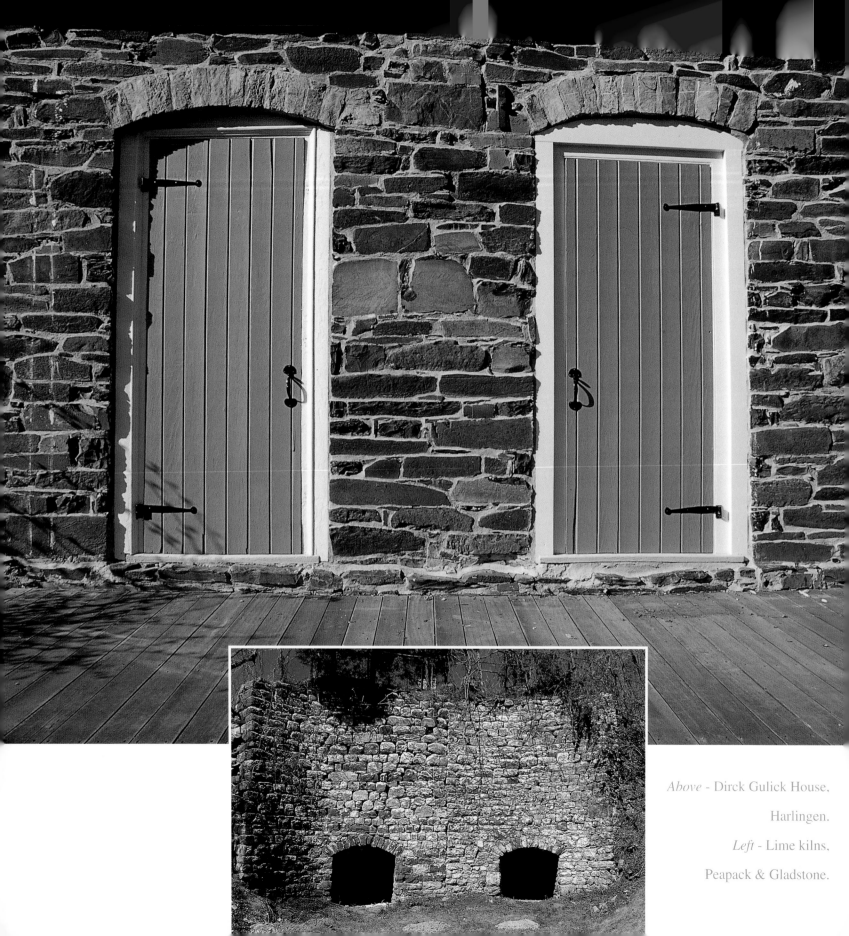

Above - Dirck Gulick House,

Harlingen.

Left - Lime kilns,

Peapack & Gladstone.

Opossum Road Bridge, 1822.

Bedens Brook, Montgomery.

Above - B & L Market,

Polish Deli, Manville.

Left - Sign, Jersey Pork Store,

North Plainfield.

Bobby B's BBQ, Somerville.

Rocky Hill flag decorates home on Washington Street.

Above - Window, The First Reformed Church, Rocky Hill.

Right - An autumn walk along Washington Street, Rocky Hill.

Somerville H.S. Jazz Band,

Municipal Building, Somerville.

Hillsborough High School

Marching Band Competition:

Top Left - Hillsborough H.S. Band.

Above - Franklin H.S. Band.

Left - Immaculata H.S. Band.

Above - North Branch General Store, Branchburg.

Opposite - Lamington General Store, Bedminster.

Overleaf - Rudolf W. van der Goot Rose Garden, Colonial Park Arboretum, Franklin.

Van Wickle House, Franklin.

Above - Texier House, Watchung.

Right - Van Horn House, Bridgewater.

Above - Horses at Lord Stirling Park, Basking Ridge.

Right - Young rider, Marissa, Hillsborough.

Opposite - Horse farm, Bedminster.

General John Frelinghuysen House,

now the Raritan Public Library, Raritan.

The Rocky Hill Community

House, Rocky Hill.

Above & Right - Borough Park,

Peapack & Gladstone.

Gazebo,

Basking Ridge.

Mt. Bethel Baptist Meeting House, 1761, Warren.

Above & Left - Young Adult Choir,
First Baptist Church of Lincoln
Gardens, Somerset.
Overleaf - Lamington River,
Burnt Mills.

Watchung Historical Site

GOD'S ACRE

HISTORIC WATCHUNG BURIAL GROUNDS

Jacob Smalley (81) Died 1836	Tabitha Smalley (41) Died 1803	Simeon Marey (46) Died 1889 *Civil War	W.L. Miray *Civil War N.J. Infantry
Abigail Smalley (66) Died 1811	Lewis James Wilson (26) Died 1858	Martha Wilson (28) Died 1858	David Demler Died 1849
Rachel Stewart (85) Died 1845	James Smalley (70) Died 1812	Zacharah Wilson (23) Died 1858	David Stewart (77) Died 1836
Mary (1yr, 9 days) Died 1859	Ann Stewart (55) Died 1848	Rhoda O. Conner Died 1818	Lewis Wilson (27) Died 1822
George Demler Died 1854	Reuben (Son of Phoebe Rynion) Died 1825	James Stewart (75) Died 1868	Henry Doty (30) Died 1797
Samuel Stewart (23) Died 1809			Mary Demler

OTHER STONES LOST

Above - Sign, historic cemetery. Watchung.

Right - Black studies historian,

William "Buzz" Hundley,

Lamington Slave Cemetery, Bedminster.

Opposite - Basking Ridge Oak in

Basking Ridge Presbyterian Cemetery.

Posing for
wedding photos,
Colonial Park,
Franklin.

Wildflowers at Ortho-McNeil
Pharmaceutical Corporation, Raritan.

Lord Memorial Fountain, 1910, Somerville.

Above - First Reformed Church, now used as
Somerset County's Jury Waiting Room, Somerville.
Left - Ann Torpey, stitching the Wallace House
commemorative quilt, Somerville.

Above - Birdwatchers at Scherman-
Hoffman Sanctuary, Bernardsville.
Left - Doris, "The Bird Lady," Bridgewater.
Opposite - Hawk, South Branch.

Above - Spillway of the new dam, Watchung.

Opposite - Stone bridge, Moorland Farms, Far Hills.

Overleaf - Raritan Valley Community College, Branchburg.

Left - Somerset Patriots manager Sparky Lyle.

Far Left & Below - Opening day ceremonies, Somerset County Ballpark, Bridgewater.

Above - Warren Lions Expo, Warren.

Top Right - Flags, Warren.

Aerial, Somerville.

Autumn aerial views:

Top Left - Far Hills.

Above - Bernardsville.

Left - Bedminster.

Statue of John Basilone,

WWII hero, Raritan.

Above - New Jersey's largest,
VFW Post 2290, Manville.

Right - 4th of July flag ceremony,
Middlebrook Encampment, Bridgewater.

Far Right - Bound Brook Drum
and Bugle Corps.

Sights along Route 22,
North Plainfield and
Green Brook.

Above - Rockingham, Washington's Headquarters in 1783, Franklin.

Opposite - Wallace House, Washington's Headquarters in 1778 and 1779, Somerville.

Overleaf - Autumn road, Far Hills.

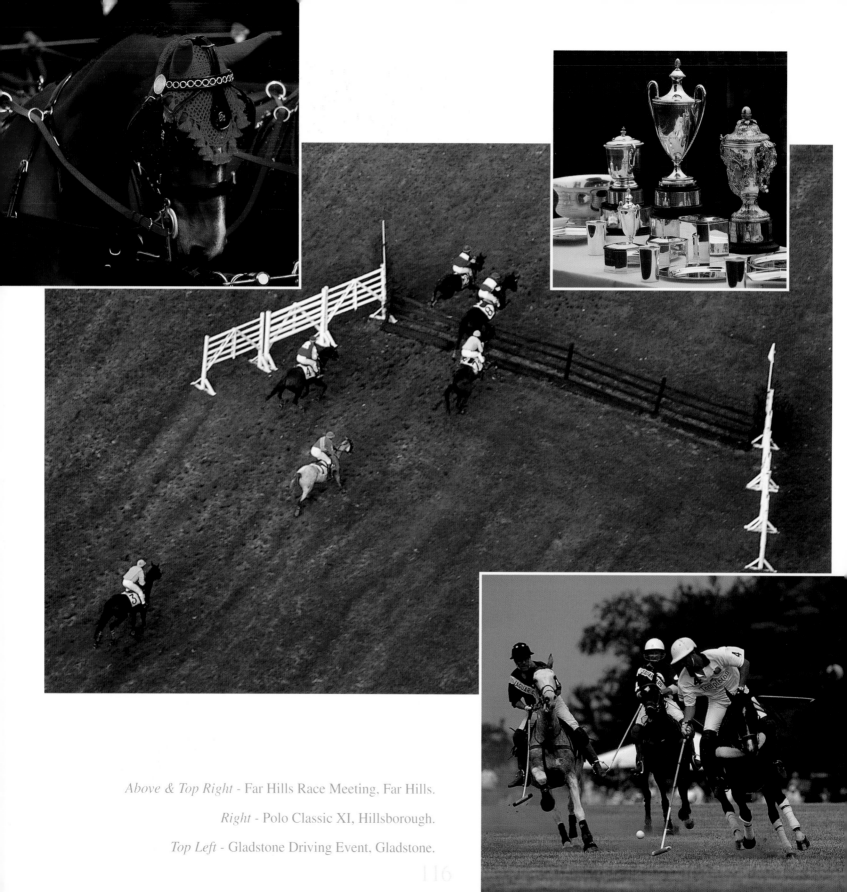

Above & Top Right - Far Hills Race Meeting, Far Hills.

Right - Polo Classic XI, Hillsborough.

Top Left - Gladstone Driving Event, Gladstone.

The Bayer / USET

Festival of Champions,

Gladstone.

St. Andrew's

Ukranian Memorial Cathedral,

South Bound Brook.

Places of worship, Bridgewater:

Top Left - Gurudwara Sahib, Sikh temple.

Above - Sri Venkateswara, Hindu temple.

Left - Temple Sholom, Jewish temple.

Overleaf - Statue of Justice atop the
Somerset County Court House, Somerville.

Somerset Alliance for the Future

The publication of this book has been a labor of love. Walter Choroszewski has shared his talent to chronicle the quality and character of the county in which he lives. Somerset Alliance for the Future made an early commitment to this project as a dedication to the quality of life and beauty of Somerset County. The Patrons, Sponsors, Contributors and Friends, who made this book possible through advance purchases, provided us with the funds necessary to complete this project on their behalf. We are grateful to The Heritage Trail Association for their support of the initiative and their assistance in marketing this book to Somerset County residents and organizations.

Somerset Alliance is unique in New Jersey and perhaps in the United States. Our formula of strong leadership, blending public and private sector representation, and focus on quality of life as the hallmark of Somerset County, with a technical staff supporting other non-profit organizations, has proven successful.

The 1990s has been a decade of unparalleled growth, countered by public acquisition of open space and farmland to preserve our countryside, and an active program of care and reinvestment in our traditional town centers. We have become the global headquarters for a select group of pharmaceutical, telecommunication, chemical and insurance enterprises. Somerset County offers diversity, a premier business location, a uniquely qualified work force and an unequaled quality of life for its residents.

*Enjoy **Somerset County, A Millennial Portrait** as a tribute to the twenty-one municipalities that make up Somerset County.*

PATRONS

Edmar Corporation / MiddleBrook Crossroads

Bound Brook

*Edmar Corporation / MiddleBrook Crossroads, owned by Marguerite Chandler
and Richmond B. Shreve, has founded numerous non-profit organizations
which serve the Somerset County community.*

Johnson & Johnson Health Care Systems, Inc.

Piscataway

*Johnson & Johnson, a founding member of Somerset Alliance for the Future,
is a proponent of community actions benefiting the quality of life
of Somerset County residents and employees.*

SPONSORS

Bridgewater Commons
Bridgewater

The Courier-News
Bridgewater

Hoechst Marion Roussel
Bridgewater

Hooper Holmes, Inc.
Basking Ridge

Johnson & Johnson Somerset County Companies
Somerset County

Lucent Technologies
Murray Hill

Pharmacia & Upjohn
Peapack & Gladstone

Somerset Coalition for Smart Growth
Somerset County

United National Bank
Bridgewater

CONTRIBUTORS

The Advance Group
Bedminster

AT&T
Basking Ridge

Bell Atlantic
Newark

The Bookworm
Bernardsville

Patrick & Mary Ann Donaghy
Bernardsville

National Starch and Chemical Company - ICI Group
Bridgewater

The Olde Mill Inn and Grain House Restaurant
Basking Ridge

PSE&G - Area Development
Newark

Marie & Fred Quick
South Branch

Romo Books
Far Hills

SJP Properties
Parsippany

Somerset County Library
Somerset County

Somerset County Park Commission
North Branch

Somerset Hills YMCA
Basking Ridge

Somerset Medical Center
Somerville

Somerset Savings Bank
Bound Brook

FRIENDS

The Advance Group
Ron Baker
The Barre Family
The Barth Family
Christopher "Kip" Bateman
Alfred & Patricia Beronio & Family
Assemblyman Peter J. Biondi
Donna & Ray Bivaletz
Leonard & Adele Blumberg
Barbara & Lou Bowers
Township of Bridgewater
Victor and Barbara Bukovecky
Allen & Linda Buurma
Caitlin Cameron and Link Leuthold
Copeland, Shimalla & Wechsler, L.L.P.
Mr. & Mrs. James Corley
Catherine Dickinson
Stephen & Judith Dragos
Dick & Mary Lou Elzer
Epic Group, Inc.
Jed & Susan Feibush
Mary Ellen Pettigrew Ferraro and Family
Flemington Car and Truck Country
Golf Event Management
Lisa M. Grech
Growth Restaurants, Inc.
Rob and Emi Hausman
Roy and Carol Higgins
T. Leonard Hill
Mr. & Mrs. Bryan Jaeger
Joanne M. Jaeger and Bruce P. McConnell
The Johnsrud Family
Alberta M. Katz
Frank & Ruth Ann Kerr
Mary & Bob King
Doug, Monique, Alex and Meaghan Krohn
Mr. & Mrs. Werner A. Kuegler
Mrs. William G. Kuhn, Jr.

Kathleen A. Kuna
Mr. & Mrs. Frederick W. Lark
Rhoda Leiman
Mr. David S. Livingston
Dr. & Mrs. James Lott
Arleen & Bill Margulis
Dr. Daniel G. Marulli
Jerry Matcho Family
Patricia A. McKiernan and Harry M. Woske, M.D.
Rosalie and David Micalchuck
Miller, Robertson & Rogers, P.C.
Henry & Jeanne Moore
Bill & Karen Munro
The Munro Family
Neshanic Garden Club
Nick & Brenda Noviello
Gerard Pascale
The Peters Family
Lenore Podraza
Dr. & Mrs. Dan C. Pullen
Arnold & Diane Van Middlesworth Radi
Raritan Valley Branch AAUW
Raritan Valley Community College
RVCC, Center for International Business & Education
Rosemary Rinehart
Thomas & Barbara Ronca & Family
Mr. & Mrs. Richard B. Shive
Mr. & Mrs. Thomas Shreve
Somerset County Planning Board
Somerset County Vocational - Technical Schools
SSP Architectural Group
Frank & Ann Torpey
United Way of Somerset County
Maxine and Norman Van Arsdale
Wabba Travel
The Wenz Family
Withum, Smith & Brown
Woolson, Sutphen, Anderson & Nergaard, P.C.